ADRENALIN RUSH

SNOWBOARDING

YVONNE THORPE

W
FRANKLIN WATTS
LONDON • SYDNEY

First published in 2011 by
Franklin Watts
338 Euston Road
London NW1 3BH

Franklin Watts Australia
Level 17/207 Kent Street
Sydney NSW 2000

Copyright © Franklin Watts 2011

Produced by Tall Tree Ltd

A CIP catalogue record for this book is available from the British Library.

Dewey Classification 796.9'39

ISBN: 978 1 4451 0477 5

Printed in China

Franklin Watts is a division of Hachette Children's Books, an Hachette UK company.

www.hachette.co.uk

Picture credits:
t–top, b–bottom, l–left, r–right, c–centre
front cover Aleksey Ipatov/Dreamstime.com, back cover jacomstephens/istockphoto.com, 1 Ben Renard-wiart/ Dreamstime.com, 4-5 Iland/ Dreamstime.com, 4bl Julia Pivovarova/ Dream-stime.com, 6–7 Sports Illustrated/Getty Images, 7br Ustyujanin/ Shutterstock, 8–9 Viappy/ Dream-stime.com, 8br Eugene Zhulkov/ Dreamstime.com, 9bl WireImage/ Getty, 10–11 Fotum / Dreamstime. com, 11tl Galyna Andrushko/ Dreamstime.com, 11tr Vanessa Morosini/ istockphoto.com, 12–13 Tudorica Alexandru/ Dreamstime.com, 13tr Lenkas/ Dreamstime.com, 13br Aaron Settipane/ Dreamstime.com, 14–15 VVO/Shutterstock, 15tl Melanie Horne/ Dreamstime.com, 16–17 Klorklor/ Dreamstime.com, 17tl Sam Downes/ Dreamstime. com, 17c Ervin Monn / Shutterstock.com, 18–19 Getty Images, 19cr Maxim Petrichuk/ Dreamstime.com, 19bl WireImage/ Getty, 20–21 Brian Finestone/ Dreamstime.com, 21tr Ben Renard-wiart/ Dreamstime.com, 21br Benis Arapovic/ Dreamstime.com, 22 Galina Barskaya/ Dreamstime.com, 23tl Monkey Business Images/ Dreamstime.com, 23bl Getty Images, 24–25 Evgeny VasenevW/ Shutterstock/ 24br Marlene Ford/ Dreamstime.com, 27br Ilya Postnikov/ Dreamstime.com, Roca / Shutterstock.com, 28bl marc fischer/istockphoto.com.

Disclaimer
The website addresses (URLs) included in this book were valid at the time of going to press. However, because of the nature of the Internet, it is possible that some addresses have changed, or sites may have changed or closed down since publication. While the author and publisher regret any inconvenience this may cause to readers, no responsibility for any such changes can be accepted either by the author or the publisher.

In preparation of this book, all due care has been exercised with regard to the advice, activities and techniques depicted. The publishers regret that they can accept no liability for any loss or injury sustained. When learning a new activity, it is important to get expert tuition and to follow a manufacturer's instructions.

Words in **bold** are in the glossary on page 30.

CONTENTS

Hurling yourself down a mountain on a snowboard is more than exciting. When you can snowboard without falling over, you will definitely look really cool on the slopes. Throw in some awe-inspiring jumps and turns, and you are set to impress!

The joy of snowboarding

What is it that makes snowboarding so popular? This snow sport is super-fun from the moment you first strap a board to your feet:

• learning – at first, you will spend most of your time falling over. But if you find some soft snow and do this with friends, even falling over can be a laugh.

• improving – pretty soon you will learn to turn. As the board slides in an easy zig-zag across the slopes, the excitement will bring a big smile to your face.

A gentle slope like this one is great for learning to snowboard.

• showing off – when you are really good, you will be able to do jumps, or carve through deep powder. The feeling of speed makes you feel like a snow-borne rocket man (or woman – this is one extreme sport where as many females as males take part).

Snowboarding world

You can snowboard anywhere there is snow. Some dedicated riders follow winter around the world, spending December to March in Europe or North America and June to September in South America or New Zealand. Others trek to icy glaciers in the middle of summer to get their boarding kicks.

After just a few weeks of learning, you could be pulling aerial tricks like this one.

Three top snowboarding movies
- The Haakonsen Faktor – *made in 1999, so a little old, this film features legendary Norwegian rider Terje Haakonsen. Shaun White (see page 13) rates this his favourite sports film ever.*
- Neverland – *this 2009 film has some of the best freeride sequences and riders around, as well as some amazing footage of urban snowboarding.*
- Lame – *ignore the title, this winner of the 2003– 2004 Snowboarder Magazine Video of the Year award is anything but lame.*

ON THE SCREEN

Snowboarding is so popular now that it is hard to imagine a time when it did not exist. But the sport is just a baby compared to skiing, its main rival on the slopes. People have been skiing for fun for more than 150 years, but snowboarding really took off only in the 1980s.

From Snurfer to snowboard

During the 1970s, a lot of people rode 'Snurfers'. The name is a combination of 'snow' and 'surfer'. The boards were like mini surfboards with leashes on the nose, which you could hold on to for balance and control. At the World Snurfer Championships in 1979, Jake Burton Carpenter turned up with a new kind of board. He had added straps that allowed him to attach the board to his boots. Today, many people recognize this as the first-ever snowboard.

Jake Burton Carpenter, sometimes called the 'Godfather of Snowboarding', riding the powder near his home in New England, USA.

Snowboard heroes: early manufacturers
- *Jake Burton Carpenter* – the Burton snowboard company was one of the first manufacturers, and today is the world's largest.
- *Tom Sims* – the skateboarder-turned-snowboarder organized the first-ever half-pipe world championship in 1983, and his company Sims produced many of the first boards.
- *Mike Olsen* – Olsen's GNU snowboard company was another of the early board manufacturers.

'Ban this dangerous sport!'

The first snowboards were hard to control and tended to go downhill wildly. Their riders were often wild, too, and it was not long before snowboarding had a bad name. It was thought that snowboarding was dangerous and that it damaged ski **runs**. Many resorts banned snowboarding, and in the mid 1980s it was allowed in fewer than one in ten ski areas. The sport refused to die out, though, and by 1990, resorts began to create separate areas for snowboarding.

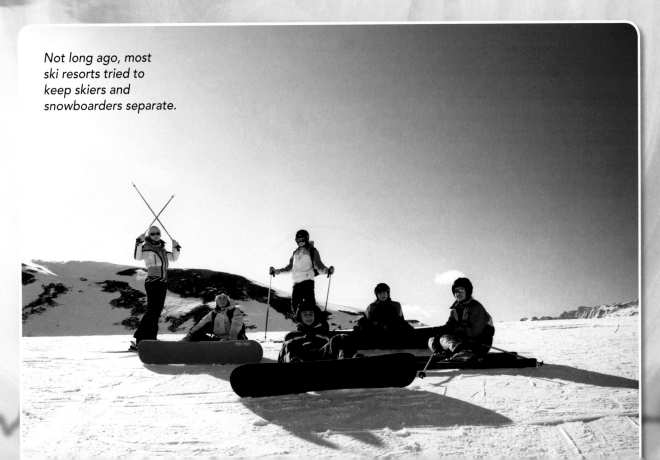

Not long ago, most ski resorts tried to keep skiers and snowboarders separate.

Snowboarding has changed a lot since the early days. Now, snowboarders are welcome just about everywhere. Not everything has changed, of course – snowboarders are still united by the thrill of sliding over snow. And on the minus side, they still have to use uncomfortable lifts designed for skiers.

Styles of snowboarding

Once they have learnt the basics, most riders specialize in a particular type of riding. The biggest division is between freestyle and freeride:

- freestylers make the most of any chance they get to become airborne or to slide their board along an obstacle. Their riding style is often influenced by skateboarding, and they practise in snow parks, which are the wintersports equivalent of skate parks. Freestylers are often found trudging to the top of a half pipe, or swooshing down it.

- freeriders are most interested in carving out big turns, riding the whole mountain from top to bottom. They do jumps but usually only when the terrain allows – for example, when the only way down is to leap off a cliff and land in the soft snow beneath. Freeriders are often found waiting for either the first or last lift of the day, hoping for a clear run at the slopes.

Deep powder snow like this is snowboarding heaven if you like off-piste freeriding.

You can see from the gouges in its side that this half pipe has been ridden by a lot of freestyle snowboarders.

Competition

There are competitions in almost all kinds of snowboarding. They range from the race you have with your friends to see who can get to the next lift fastest, to 'extreme' contests for getting down a whole mountain in the most spectacular way. At the Winter Olympics, there are boardercross races (see page 18) and half pipe contests (see page 16).

Cara-Beth Burnside was one of the first women to show that female riders can be just as awesome in the half pipe as men. Originally a skateboarder (and winner of Female Skater of the Year in 2003), she is one of a tiny group of people who have won gold medals at both Summer and Winter **X-Games**.

CARA-BETH BURNSIDE

Snowboarding equipment is pretty simple – a board, boots and bindings. There are lots of different styles, from **swallow-tail** powder boards to step-in bindings. The main difference is between freestyle- and freeride-based equipment.

Buying a board

If you are new to boarding, you might want to rent a board at first. Once you know what kind of equipment suits you, it might be a good idea to buy your own. Shop assistants will be able to give you advice on which board suits your riding style best.

Boards often have a wooden core with plastic covering the top and underside. There are screw holes on top to attach the bindings.

Thin metal strips, called edges, run down the outside of the bottom. These are used to help the board grip into the snow while turning or stopping.

Boots are designed to be stiff enough to keep their shape during turns, and are padded so that they are comfortable to wear all day.

Bindings hold the boot to the board. Strap bindings, which grip the toe and ankle areas, are most common.

A short, lightweight board makes spins and tricks in the air easier.

Types of board

There are two basic types of board, boot and binding:

- freestyle equipment – for freestyle, people often ride shorter boards that come up to their chins when stood upright. These boards are **double-ended**. Boots tend to be less stiff to make twisting and spinning easier.

- freeride equipment – freeride boarders use a longer board (up to their nose), and the nose (front) of the board is usually longer than the **tail**.

You could go boarding in shorts and a T-shirt (and some people do in spring). But when the chairlift stops moving because a sudden storm has closed in, you WILL regret it – if you do not freeze! Having the right clothes and equipment makes snowboarding much more enjoyable, and safer, too.

Snowboard clothes

The key to dressing for boarding is to wear layers so you can strip off a layer or two if you get hot. Standard kit for snowboarding includes:

- thermal base layer, which draws away sweat and keeps you warm.

- trousers, often with side-zips that can be opened if you get too hot. The best ones are waterproof with reinforced areas on the knees and bottom. They also have elasticated cuffs that fit over your boots.

- thin fleece, ideally with a full-length zip for cooling down and a high collar for keeping your neck warm.

- jacket, usually with a **snow skirt**.

In a crash like this one, a snow skirt inside your jacket stops snow being slooshed into areas where it should not sloosh!

Other equipment

All riders wear gloves to keep their hands warm and dry. Many snowboarders also ride wearing a helmet, goggles and a small backpack (see below).

Snowboarding goggles stop the glare of the white snow damaging your eyes.

Helmet
Rarely compulsory, but as moves become increasingly trickier, more riders are choosing to wear them.

Backpack
Inside their backpack, most riders will have the following:
- *spare clothes.*
- *survival blanket and mobile phone in case of an accident. Off-piste riders also carry **avalanche** gear, such as **avalanche reflectors**.*
- *multi-tool to make repairs and adjustments to the snowboard and the bindings.*
- *drinks to keep hydrated. Keep drinks in a soft plastic bottle, not a hard metal one.*
- *snacks in case of hunger and/or disaster.*

Sometimes called 'The Flying Tomato' because of his red hair, Shaun White is probably the best half pipe snowboarder the world has ever seen. He is the winner of multiple X-Games gold medals (as well as a silver for skateboarding), but his biggest wins were at the Olympic Games. White won gold at the 2006 Turin Olympics, then again at the 2010 Vancouver Games.

SHAUN WHITE

Most boarders ride in ski resorts, where there are lifts that will take them to the top of the slope. Most of the time they then slide back downhill on a piste, which is a specially prepared area of smoothed-out snow, free of obstacles.

Piste markers and grades

Pistes are usually marked out with tall poles on either side of the slope. Even in heavy snow when it is hard to see, boarders and skiers can pick their way carefully down the mountain by following these poles.

In almost all the world's ski resorts, pistes are graded according to difficulty. In Europe, the grades start with an easy green (in France only), then progress through blue, red and black. In North America the basic grades go green, blue and black.

Lifts were designed with forwards-facing skiers in mind, rather than sideways-riding snowboarders. As a result, they are often a very uncomfortable experience.

Your first go on a button lift like this one can be a humbling experience. People quickly get the hang of them, though.

Lifts

After sliding to the bottom of a slope, boarders hitch a ride back uphill on a ski lift. There are three main kinds of ski lift:

- cable cars and bubbles are the easiest to get on and off and the most comfortable.

- chair lifts are easy-ish to get on and off, but they force you to twist round uncomfortably to sit down.

- drag lifts, such as button lifts, are hard to use and uncomfortable. They are a sign that a resort does not pay much attention to the needs of snowboarders!

Top snowboard mobile phone games
- Snowboard Hero – *a great basic game, with the chance to perform all kinds of mid-air tricks as you leap and slide your way down a choice of courses.*
- Extreme Air Snowboarding – *the great tutorial mode will soon have you ripping it up in the virtual half pipe.*
- X2 Snowboarding – *one of the most popular snowboard games, which boasts brilliant control and customization, and exciting racecourses.*

Many riders quickly find that simply sliding downhill is not enough for them. They want to make their friends gasp in amazement at their acrobatic skills. They want to make onlookers cheer at their bravery. They want to pull jaw-dropping tricks that will push them to the limit. They want, in two words, BIG AIR.

A rider gets big air off a purpose-built ramp in Val d'Isere in the French Alps.

Half pipes and high jumps

There are various ways to get airborne on a snowboard. You can even **pop** a little **ollie** (a small jump) while riding along flat ground. But to get high, you need a ramp. The bigger the ramp, the higher you can go. Skilled riders put together incredibly spectacular routines on half pipes.

A half pipe is a U-shaped ramp, just like those seen at a skate park. Competition riders have to concentrate on making one long, smooth run, usually with six or more jumps, rather than doing a single huge aerial. The half pipe is not where the biggest jumps are seen.

Quarter pipes and higher jumps

A quarter pipe is half of a half pipe. The riders get a long run-up (sometimes towed behind a snowmobile for maximum speed), then launch vertically into the air. They get one chance, and all they have to do is land safely. In 2007, at the age of 33, Terje Haakonsen set a new world record for a quarter-pipe jump of 9.8 metres above the top of the ramp.

Spectators crane their necks backwards to try to keep a big air competitor in view.

Snowboarding legend Kevin Pearce at the Open Snowboarding Championships in Laax, Switzerland, in 2009.

Air and Style
This is an annual aerial contest currently held in Innsbruck, Austria (it has also been held in Munich, Germany). The riders leap from a giant jump, performing their best tricks while airborne. Past champions have included some of snowboarding's greats: Ingmar Backmann, Terje Haakonsen, Stefan Gimpl, Shaun White, Travis Rice and Kevin Pearce.

KNOW THE FACTS

Boardercross was one of the biggest hits of the 2010 Winter Olympics in Vancouver, Canada. This might have been because it features many crashes and embarrassing mistakes, even by some of the world's best riders!

Competitors head for the line at the end of a boardercross contest. The blue line marks the edge of the run.

Side-by-side racing

Boardercross is a knockout competition. In each round, four riders race side-by-side over a series of jumps and obstacles. There is usually only one fast way down the course, and with four riders trying to fit themselves into it, things can become messy. The first two across the finishing line go through to the next round; the last two go home.

The boardercross style of competition is so popular that it has been 'borrowed' by skiing. Skiercross is now one of the most popular spectator events on the ski calendar.

Boardercross courses

The course normally opens with a start gate. As soon as this opens, the riders come flying out, trying to pick up as much speed as possible. Then there will be a series of banked-up bends, which test the riders' ability to corner at speed. There are always a few jumps, too – sometimes really big ones. On beginners' courses you can usually ride around these or go over them slowly, but this takes a lot longer.

Whether you ride regular (left foot first) or goofy (right foot first), there will be some turns on a boardercross course that suit you – and some that do not...

The US rider Lindsey Jacobellis is famous for two things: being one of the best female boardercross riders, and being one of the unluckiest. At the 2006 Olympics, Jacobellis was safely in the lead when, going into the last-but-one jump, she crashed on landing, and by the time she had got up could only finish second. 'Snowboarding is fun,' she later said, 'I was having fun.'

Once riders have mastered the basic skills of snowboarding (going in a straight line and turning), they start adding some extra thrills in the form of freestyle tricks. Most experts have at least a handful of these that they can throw in at a split-second's notice, if the terrain gives them the chance.

This boarder is performing an indy grab, with the leading arm thrown out behind for good measure.

Freestyle tricks

Snowboarding has a whole bunch of tricks and they sometimes sound like a whole different language: a 'McTwist', for example, is a 'forward-flipping backside 540 with a grab'. But most tricks are made up of just three things – jumps, spins and grabs:

• jumps – a simple jump can be done off purpose-built ramps, or from bumps in the surface of the snow. Lots of people learn these using the little built-up areas at the edges of a piste.

• spins – these add difficulty to a jump. Twisting round through 180 degrees while in the air, for example, means riders land 'fakie' – with the tail of the board in front.

- grabs – This is when you grab the nose, tail or rail of the board while in the air. The most basic grab is an 'indy', which involves grabbing the toe edge of the board between your feet using your trailing hand.

Expert freestyle boarders throw other moves into their routines, including:

- grinds – grinds involve boarders sliding their boards along handrails, roofs and fallen trees.

- rolls – a roll is an experts-only move. Rolls involve getting upside-down, or 'inverted', while airborne. They are considered so dangerous that they have been banned in some competitions.

Freestyle aerial skills can come in handy when you are riding off-piste, too.

Two top snow parks
- *Copper Mountain, Colorado, USA – regularly voted one of North America's best snow parks, with something for every ability level.*
- *Snow Park, New Zealand – no prizes for imaginative naming, but this is a good place to spot some of the world's top freestyle snowboarders during the southern hemisphere winter.*

In the early days of snowboarding, if you wanted to snowboard, you had to do it away from marked runs. Today, many boarders still enjoy the feeling of ignoring the piste markers and finding their own way down the mountain. In Europe, this is known as off-piste riding, while in North America it is called backcountry.

A rider jumps for joy while flying high over backcountry.

Experts only!

Freeriders need impressive skills because they have to be able to deal with whatever the mountain throws at them. A 5-metre cliff? They will have to jump it, or stop in time to **backtrack**. Deep powder? Keep the nose of the board up, or dig themselves out. Thick forest? Make sure their turning technique is up to scratch!

Off-piste hazards

Snowboarding away from marked runs is dangerous. Deep snow can hide all kinds of hazards, such as rocks, deep holes and fallen trees. Away from the areas that have been made safe by specialist workers called pisteurs, there is always a danger that you could set off an avalanche.

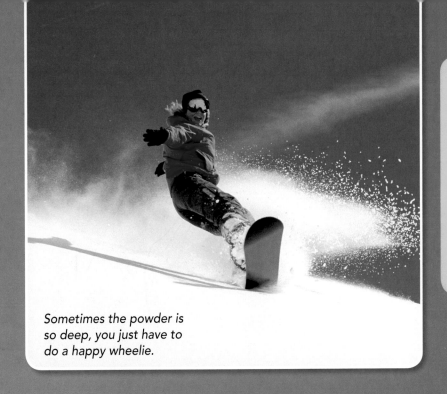

Sometimes the powder is so deep, you just have to do a happy wheelie.

Ride with a guide

The best way to ride off-piste is with a local guide. Guides can be hired for an hour or two, half a day or a whole day. The main reasons for riding with a guide are:
- they know the areas where it is safe.
- they can take you on the best, most secret routes.
- a guide will stop you going down a valley or slope that looks inviting but, just out of sight, turns into a river valley with no way out except to walk back up the mountain.

Travis Rice was born and lives in Jackson Hole, one of the USA's top freeride locations. His riding combines the massive jumps and wild settings of freeriding with the technical skills of freestyle. Much in demand from filmmakers, Rice's most famous jump is probably a switch 540 performed while jumping the 37-metre-wide Chad's Gap in Utah.

Snowboarding is good for you. It makes your heart and lungs stronger, improves coordination and balance, and introduces you to places you might not otherwise see. But snowboarding is also a dangerous sport. Every year riders are seriously injured, or even killed.

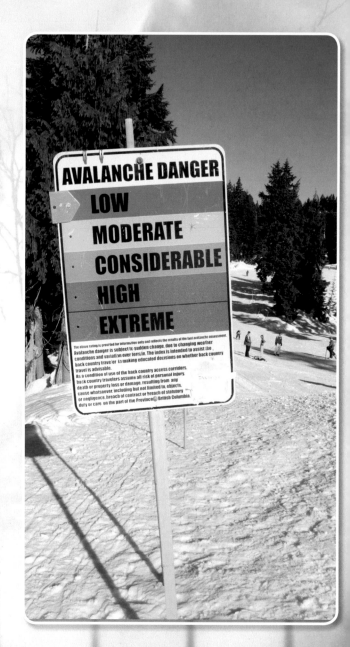

ALWAYS take heed of the avalanche warnings, and avoid areas where there is a risk of avalanches.

Stay safe

These simple things can make snowboarding safer:

- check your gear – make sure that all the screws and bolts on your bindings are done up tightly. They are under massive pressure, and one popping off can be disastrous.

- wear a helmet – break an arm or leg and, a few months later, most people will have made a full recovery. Head injuries are different and can be fatal.

- go at your own speed – it can be tempting to try to keep up with better riders but once you are moving too fast, things can go wrong more quickly than you would expect. Before you know it, you could be crashing into a tree you would normally be able to avoid.

Piste rules

Snow sports resorts are often crowded, with people of all abilities sharing the slopes. To make things safer, snowboarders and skiers have come up with a few simple guidelines:

- *The downhill person has right of way. This means that if you are further up the slope, you must safely avoid people below you as you overtake them. If you cannot overtake safely, slow down.*
- *Never stop in the middle of the piste, or just over the brow of a slope where other riders cannot see you, for a picnic or a chat. Pull over to the side, where you will not be in anyone's way.*
- *Snowboarders must always wear a **leg leash**, so that their board cannot slide off down the slope and injure someone.*

- do not go, unless you know the way – just because another boarder has taken a particular route, that does not make it safe to follow them. The other boarder might be much more experienced than you – or he or she could have crashed just around the corner!

This rider has got caught up at the edge of a small avalanche. Even a small one like this will contain tonnes of snow, rock and ice.

You can snowboard wherever there is snow and a slope. Of course, it helps if someone has built a lift to take you uphill. And it is even better if they have planned out a whole load of runs for you. But where would you go snowboarding if you won an aeroplane ticket to travel anywhere in the world? Here are some ideas:

Tien Shan in central Asia provides some great riding for adventurous snowboarders.

Whistler Blackcomb, Canada

Deep, reliable snowfall, modern lifts and a giant snowboard area that offers good riding for everyone, from beginners to experts – it is no wonder Whistler Blackcomb is often rated as one of the world's best resorts.

Jackson Hole, USA

Jackson Hole has the biggest **vertical drop** of any resort in North America. It is one of the best resorts on the continent (and probably the world) for riding steep, deep, fresh powder. There are also two snow parks and a half pipe for freestylers.

Verbier, Switzerland

One of Europe's oldest ski resorts, this is the place to head for some of the best snowboarding through trees in Europe.

Queenstown, New Zealand

The adventure sports capital of New Zealand, Queenstown has a massive variety of riding, from gentle slopes for beginners to some of the world's best heli-boarding.

Chamonix, France

For experienced off-piste riders, Chamonix is heaven. For anyone else, it is not so much fun. The extreme, steep slopes and regular falls of fresh snow mean that a hard core of riders spend the whole winter here.

Åre, Sweden

Pronounced 'ore-uh', Åre is so far north that in the middle of the winter, you need floodlights to find your way around the snow park. But at the end of the season, in May, the sun barely sets. If you want to snowboard in the light of the midnight sun, this is the place.

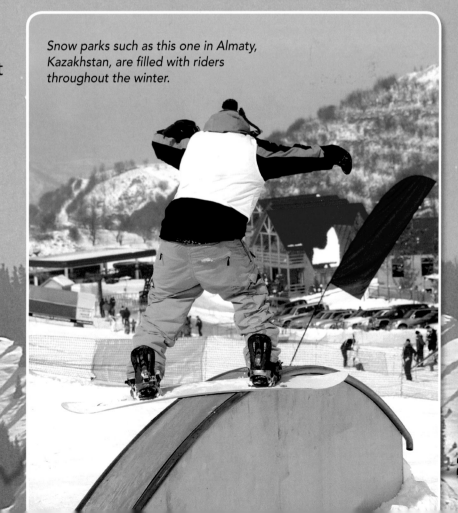

Snow parks such as this one in Almaty, Kazakhstan, are filled with riders throughout the winter.

Some snowboarders really do not like crowds. They gave up piste riding years ago. Even the popular off-piste areas have started to seem a bit too busy. What they really enjoy is having an entire mountain all to themselves (and perhaps a few friends). This is the world of extreme snowboarding.

Living the dream

Imagine this: you and a few others load your boards on the helicopter's rack and climb in. The pilot takes off, and flies you to the top of an **untracked** slope of fresh powder. The drop-off point might be so small that the pilot cannot actually land: you may have to jump out of the chopper with your board!

The reward, however, is the ride down, through fresh snow, with no lift noises, no skiers, beginners to slow down for, or other distractions. At the bottom, the chopper is waiting to take you to the next drop-off.

This dream actually exists: it is called heli-boarding, and can be done in many resorts. In other places, snowmobiles are used in the same way, to take riders to out-of-the-way locations. This can be a good option if you are not a millionaire, as it is much cheaper than heli-boarding.

Using a snowmobile to get up a mountain is pretty good fun.

Remote locations

Some riders have started exploring places where snowboarding and skiing have never been done before. They have to trek there using **snowshoes** or mountain-climbing boots with **crampons**. The amount of effort and equipment involved means that only a few expeditions like this take place each year.

Three top heli-boarding spots
- *Valdez, Alaska, USA – possibly the spiritual home of heli-boarding, the Valdez Mountains offer some of the deepest, most reliable powder around.*
- *Queenstown, New Zealand – famous as an adrenaline-junkie's kind of town. In the winter you can get your fix by taking a helicopter to New Zealand's Southern Alps.*
- *Zermatt, Switzerland – Switzerland is probably the best country in Europe for heli-boarding, and Zermatt is surrounded by some extremely high mountains, including the world-famous Matterhorn.*

A short helicopter ride will take you to the parts of a mountain that ski lifts just cannot reach.

avalanche
slide of huge amounts of snow down a mountainside.

avalanche reflectors
special patches, sewn into ski clothing and backpacks, which reflect radio waves and allow rescue teams to detect people trapped beneath snow.

backtrack
go back the way you came. This usually means walking back up the mountain.

crampons
spiky attachments for the soles of a boot, which allow it to grip well on ice and snow.

double-ended
the same at both ends.

leg leash
device for attaching your leg to a snowboard.

ollie
jump done from level ground, using the rider's speed and leg strength to get off the ground.

pop
to perform suddenly.

runs
another name for pistes.

snow skirt
inner layer of a snowboarding and skiing jacket, which is tightened around the hips to keep snow from going up inside the jacket during a fall.

snowshoes
wide, lightweight platforms that can be strapped to your shoes to make it easier to walk across snow.

swallow-tail
board with a tail that has two pointed tips.

tail
rear end of a snowboard.

untracked
without any signs of other snowboarders having passed.

vertical drop
distance from the top of the highest piste to the bottom of the lowest.

X-Games
annual extreme sports competition with versions for both winter and summer sports.

Competitions and organizations

The biggest snowboarding competitions are the World Cup, the X-Games and the Olympic Games.

The World Cup is a season-long set of competitions, which decides who are the best riders over the whole year. There are several different categories, including Big Air, Boardercross and Half Pipe. To find a World Cup event near you, go to www.fissnowboard.com.

The X-Games are held in the USA every year, and they attract the world's top snowboarders. There are also regional versions of the X-Games, for example in Europe.

The Olympics is run by the IOC (International Olympic Committee). Go to www.olympic.org and click on 'Snowboarding' for information about past medalists and the history of the sport.

Online magazines

http://fresh.snowboardermag.com
Online resource of the US print magazine *Snowboarder*, with excellent articles about travel locations, equipment, techniques and top snowboarders. Also has a good 'Videos' section.

http://whitelines.mpora.com
The online world of *Whitelines* snowboard magazine from the UK, this also has interviews, equipment and techniques, plus videos. A good take on the European snowboarding scene.

www.boardtheworld.com
A purely online magazine, with excellent coverage of the international competition scene. Also carries resort information for just about every resort you can think of.

INDEX

These are the lists of contents for each title in Adrenalin Rush:

Snowboarding

Hitting the slopes • The birth of snowboarding • Snowboarding today • Snowboard design • Equipment and clothing • Piste riding • Big air • Boardercross • Riding freestyle • Freeriding fun • Staying alive • Snowboard hotspots • Extreme snowboarding

MTB

Hit the dirt • Pioneers of MTB • MTB conquers the world • Types of bike • Equipment and clothing • Cross-country • Cross-country racing • Long-haul heroes • North Shore style • Four-cross • Downhill racers • Staying alive • Mountain bike hotspots

BMX

One gear is plenty • BMX takes over the world • The rebirth of BMX • Bike love • Equipment and clothing • Street riding • Ramps and vert riding • Flatland skills • Dirt jumping • BMX racing • Racetrack skills • Staying alive • BMX hotspots

Skateboarding

Hitting the concrete • Pioneers of skating • Conquering the world • Board meeting • Equipment and clothing • Street skating • Ramping up • Vert and mega ramps • Flatland tricks • Longboard riding • Going downhill – fast! • Staying alive • Skateboard hotspots